I0756335

FINISHING LINE PRESS
www.finishinglinepress.com

The Third Remembrance

poems by

Jayne Brown

Finishing Line Press
Georgetown, Kentucky

The Third Remembrance

ISBN 979-8-89990-399-1 First Edition

ACKNOWLEDGMENTS

"If We Could Marry" and "Just a Couple of Old Women Having their Wedding Photos Done in Central Park" were published in *CALYX: A Journal of Art and Literature By Women*
"The Patient Presents" and "Out Here on these Cliffs" were published in *Gyroscope Review*
"My Tomboy" was first performed by the author for the "Five Minute Fringe Fest" in Reading, PA
Note: The final stanza of "Late Winter Altar, Waiting," is a variation on the Metta (Lovingkindness) meditations.

Publisher: Leah Huete de Maines
Editor: Christen Kincaid
Cover Art: Jayne Brown
Author Photo: Janice Chernekoff
Cover Design: Elizabeth Maines McCleavy

Order online: www.finishinglinepress.com
also available on amazon.com

Author inquiries and mail orders:
Finishing Line Press
PO Box 1626
Georgetown, Kentucky 40324
USA

Contents

In fond remembrance of my parents,
Dorothy Jayne and Francis L. Relaford

From The Five Remembrances:

I am of the nature to grow old. There is no way to escape growing old.

I am of the nature to have ill health. There is no way to escape ill health.

I am of the nature to die. There is no way to escape death.

From an ancient Pali Text attributed to the Buddha

My Tomboy

At seventy, I want back my Tomboy.
At ten, I was not so much
a Daddy's Girl as Mom's Boy.
I was her sidekick, riding shotgun,
shunning lipstick for a denim jacket
and a ball cap, a yearly pixie cut,
and cutoffs sticking down below
school's mandatory skirt.

Not Queen for a Day, but my Own Queen,
Prince of my Life. I used the wand
from mother's Maybelline
to brush a dashing mustache on.
I didn't so much want to be a boy
as brave, and strong—the first girl
in the major leagues. Or Peter Pan.
I'd stand like Mary Martin
in the full-length mirror—
arms akimbo, fists on hips,
belting out, "I Won't Grow Up!"
and "I've Gotta Crow!"

I'd stare into those bathroom mirrors,
dreaming all that I could be. Then: puberty.
It got me lost, tossed off somewhere.
I traded pixie cuts for long hair
ironed into curtains for my face,
replaced the cutoff jeans with miniskirts,
tight shirts, halter tops, and chokers
I would macrame.

I should know better now, but why
do all my sentences still end with questions?
Why do I still buffer my suggestions,
and giggle like a girl when I am nervous?
What does this service?

I watched my mother, late in life,
give up “nice” for strong.
She stood up in her church to say
that people like her daughter
and her granddaughter belong.

I want them back—my tomboy-self, my mom.
I want a comeback as her sidekick,
want to trade outdated fears for Tomboy spirit.

Sweetheart

It surprised me when I called you that.
"Sweetheart." Not Mommy or Mother. Sweetheart.
"Sweetheart, you are doing so good."

And you were—light years ahead of me,
bent into your center, hunkered down
like a woman in labor,
deep in the thick, hard work
to deliver yourself
from your (well) spent body.

Daddy used to whistle that song to you,
even sing it to you sometimes.
"Let Me Call you Sweetheart,"
on our long trips through the southwest—
Zion, Bryce, the Painted Desert—
while we sat reading, rolling our eyes in the back seats
of the big-finned Ford, the Plymouth Fury.

And maybe he's waiting in the wings
to croon his tune to you again.
Long ago not long ago I told his ghost,
"You can't have her yet."
But you're not ours anymore.
You're gone beyond,
almost gone to the other shore.

You woke up once and said,
"I have to make this movie stop."
I stood to turn the TV off,
then realized you meant everything.

We flickered there in black and white,
waiting to be gone beyond.
One of us bent and whispered,
"It's okay, Mom. You can let go."

From your still body came
 your still-strong voice—
"I'm not going anywhere!"

Oh, Sweetheart! Sweetheart,
let me call you that.

Palinode to Weather-Talk

for my father

You hold the cordless, circumnavigate
the driveway, watering geraniums
you don't recall you watered yesterday.
That's what you call it—*circumnavigate*—
a word you're pleased to put your tongue around.

You're like our old cat who used to piss us off
by sneaking up and drinking from our water cups.
The one who, now she's dying, has a special glass
we keep topped up.

All your life,
we finished sentences for you, we rushed you,
wife and daughters talking circles all around you,
we let the real talk stop when you walked in:
"Hello there."
"Is it hot out?"
"Did you take your insulin?"

Now that every sentence hides a dozen snares,
each phrase a maze or thicket to get lost inside,
we wait in silence as you fumble toward the end.

Once I scorned our weather-talk, thought of it
like *naugahyde, formica*—fake,
a sign of everything we'd circumnavigate
to keep things safe. Now that past and future
have abandoned you, and nouns, tell me
"Morning fog" and "Sunshine" for as long as we have left.

Let our little dialogues repeat themselves so faithfully
they wear a path for you to find your way along,
a route as clear as the two black lines
that mark your night-time shuffling track
from bedroom to the bathroom door and back.

Whistler's Daughter

I loved you easiest from the back seat,
riding home after Starlight Opera musicals,
your suit coat, scratchy as your whiskers,
sideways over me, my legs tucked in to fit,
pretending sleep as streetlights passed,
as the moon kept pace, as you whistled
show tunes the whole way home.

As years went on, I wanted words,
but learned to recognize your pride
in how a dimple deepened in your cheek,
your happiness from how your chin tucked in,
the way you rocked a little on your heels.
Your love I learned from whistled songs.
You'd serenade our mother as you drove:
"Daisy, Daisy, Give me your answer true…."

Now you are a blue jay feather in the grass,
the wind chime in the weeping cherry tree.
I see you in a gladiola's bright orange blossom spike,
in my own old body bending forward,
just like yours, with seedlings and a trowel.

If I asked a medium to conjure you,
I'd know it was really you
if there were no words—
only her surprised eyes
and her puckered lips
warbling out a love song
from a Broadway show
she didn't even know.

Some enchanted evening
if you came through,
every note from you
would find its way to true,
like the open longing
from a slide guitar,
like the bending weeping
of a singing saw.

Losing It

After "One Art" by Elizabeth Bishop

Yesterday I didn't recognize my purse.
Last year, I didn't recognize my friend.

To be fair, the purse was nondescript, the friend
wore makeup and a dress, had contacts in.

I'd never liked that purse. Plain black vinyl, cheap,
it works. But I had always loved my friend.

I know I'm not the first to fear the worst,
to wait for senior moments that don't end,

for lapses that extend to loss of words, abyss, or worse.
My father finally didn't recognize his house.

My mother learned to lie, to leave and come back in
with a cheery "Dear, I'm home!" in hopes of jogging him.

I hope that's not my portion of the family curse.
I cannot change my chromosomal blend.

Just in case, I'm learning to pretend.
I've armed myself with fillers, *what's-his-face* and *thingy*, to stick in.

I've bought myself a purple purse. I've been forgiven by my friend.
There is no art to losing it, no thing to master to blend in

if that disaster's destined to descend. Near the end,
he only knew his mother and his brothers, all long passed.

And if I'm heading toward the cliff-edge of that curse,
I'll hope to see my parents' ghosts toward the end.

My Grandson Says He's Skibidi

and I say, "You're what, Honey?"
Skibidi—it sounds like happiness,
like skipping down the road
to "Zippity Do-Dah" or
"Bibbidi-Bobbidi-Boo,"
so I say to him, "I'm skibidi, too,
when I'm with you."
"Silly Ama!" he laughs.
"You're Skibidi Ohio!"

Turns out skibidi is either good or weird,
or both. Next day he says, "I'm Rizz!"
Now, Rizz I can remember
as the downbeat in "charisma,"
and the way he strokes his jawline
with a saucy sideways glance.

Shoot, he was rizz in nursery school,
and knew it, too, the girls all hanging
on the chain link fence for a first glance
when he walked in. They waved to him
and sang, "Good morning, Jeremiah!"

He's all Gen Alpha now at ten.
I tried his shoes on—my feet swim in them.
He has his Youtube channels, plural.
He loops tracks, writes raps, lays down beats,
makes videos, stop-action animation.

He's not just skibidi or rizz,
he's irony and kindness too.
He knows what's fair, and cares.
He has an aura, and he's delta.
He knows almost everything is sus.

He's ready for this brain-rot century,
for the current resident of the presidency
who he sees as Beta, as completely cringe,
a bad dad joke, and just dismisses him.

He knows a kid can be an influencer too,
can have a platform, transform, perform,
have tons of followers and build his brand,
can make his niche, and make it through,
and I hope and pray that's exactly what he'll do.

The Patient Presents

"The patient presents as a pleasant, obese 70-year-old woman."
Doctor's notes

The physician presents
as a middle-aged man-boy,
balding, beefy, if not obese,
baffled a bit by his middle-age.

Likely good at video games,
the physician likes his surgeries fast,
enjoys the Gameboy aspect of his craft.
Enamored of his lightning moves
as he threads his way
through femoral arteries
and into the heart,
he revs it up with a little shock,
and deploys the payload
with its pig valve inside.

The physician remembers
to include concern
during patient appointments.
Does she have someone
who can take her home,
who will look after her
till she's back on her feet?

"Yes," she smiles. "My wife
will be there."
He barely blanches,
she'll grant him that.

And while no other man
has made her heart race
in fifty-plus years,
the patient presents as listening intently,
avidly smiling, nodding, impressed.

She wishes him God-speed,
wishes him skilled.
She hopes he's at least
as good as he thinks,
as he explains what he'll do
in minute detail.

What I Missed Most in the Pandemic

I longed to browse again someday.
I wanted to browse just like it sounds—
a round, drowsy sound, loose in the body,
easy on the mind. To hang around, to be somewhere,
loafing and leaning for hours and hours.

Then, even The Browser's Bookshop was closed.
Everything felt flat—a life reduced to lists,
as dull as dish soap or disposable gloves,
as cold and bland as sanitizer on your hands.

I wanted to wander down aisles again,
to squat on the floor of Firefly Books,
thumb open a cover and read the first page,
breathe those old paper smells of vanilla and sage.

Or to gently rock the shopping cart
as I worked my way down aisles of shirts,
fondling the fabric, gauging the drape,
letting my brain go blissfully blank.

To lift a cantaloupe and feel its heft,
admire its webbing, the blush underneath,
to push in its little umbilicus,
and bring that melon up to my face.
To pause, and inhale its musky grace.

If We Could Marry

Written June, 2010, when we couldn't

If we could marry, and if we did,
I'd come to you with bare white head.
You'd stand with me despite your knees
under an arch we'd weave from our apple trees.

I'd give up hoping you'd wear a tux.
You'd give up hoping I'd give this all up.
And our friends would be there to wish us luck
    If we could marry.

If we could marry, and if we did,
You'd bake white cake, I'd bake black bread.
You'd cook up a soup while I picked the greens.
We'd set out the chairs and ready the scene
    If we could marry.

When everyone had headed home
and you and I were left alone,
we'd wash the dishes, wrap up the bread,
and lie down to sleep in our same old bed.

And everything would be the same.
Nothing—Everything—nothing would change
    If we could marry.

Just a Couple of Old Women Getting Their Wedding Photos Done in Central Park

Summer, 2014

The locals flick their gazes past us and away.
Two women's no big deal here, even posing,
pinkies linked or hands crisscrossed, exposing
new gold bands, years late, exchanged today.

Not famous, young, or fabulous enough
for second looks, we're legal—and so pleased we
strike each pose, however weird or cheesy,
our friend asks for, hoping magic's in her proofs.

And there! In one, she's made our bodies form one heart
that starts where our two foreheads press, then arcs
around our gray (say silver!) heads, shorn short,
and meets at the top buttons of our shirts.

Somehow she's caught a golden light that's set
our faces shining, and our eyes alight.

Out Here on the Cliffs

The young woman, a girl really, steps out
past the boundaries here on the cliffs.
Past the warning signs, the flagstone walls,
the swinging chain she scissors across.
Where the slippery shale slides down the slope,
where the hard winds buffet in sudden gusts,
and the wild surf gobbles the sandstone below,
she stands and lifts herself into a pose.

Willowy, young, she's all thin stems, all relevés
and flexible bends. She's become a swan,
from her slipper-shod feet to the tilt of her head.
Up through her thick, luscious pleated silk skirt
—she'd call it vintage, a year I remember—
through her fitted jacket, to her throat that extends,
like a heron, a crane, without craning her neck,
everything's smooth and curved and long,
from the curtain of satin composing her hair
to the brilliant eye turned up to the sky.

Now I see the young man she's brought to be camera,
see how clearly she pictures herself.
So much beauty, so much youth—
all hers to squander, hers to destroy.

We shake our heads and file past.
Busloads of grey-heads treading the path.
Nobody calls to her, "Young Lady, Get back!"
Why bother? She doesn't feel mortal yet,
can not imagine her body broken,
dashed to bits on the rocks below.

We shake our heads and turn away.
We do not want to see her fall today.
Knowing the body is all too perishable,
we're glad for the barriers, glad for

our windbreakers, our sensible shoes,
just glad to be walking out this far
over the ocean on grass-covered cliffs.
Glad for the slabs of slate almost as tall as us,
even the electrified cattle fence
that marks the end of the public land
and keeps us mindful of the narrow path,
away from the dangers of looking down,
or looking back, of remembering when
we used to love skirting our deaths.

So Here We Are

So here we are now at the edge of the cliff,
no one in front to take the brunt.
The Greatest Generation, gone.
Now it's us next up, their kids—the ones
with every chance, all the potential
we never lived up to, never quite met.

In the sixties, we were stardust.
Glorious, golden, we believed it,
became emboldened, blew barriers open.
Now we're olden.

"Back in your day," my students would say,
as if I was frozen, a dinosaur, Lincoln.
Back then we spilled out, a carload of girls
on opening night of *2001*.

"Could we still be alive then?" one of us asked.
A collective gasp as we did the math.
"We'll be so old then—almost 50!"
Oh, Fifty! My children are fifty.

We could stand at this drop-off for many more years
before our turn in the churning waves.
We shift in our shoes, and gravel rolls off the cliff,
quietly sprinkles the beach down below.

Practicing Corpse Pose

As a girl, I'd pretend that my bed was a raft
that carried me over from daytime to dream.
The boat and my body, the wake that we left,
washed us away down an underground stream.

Now thought trickles off in this pose of a death,
and bridges the worlds of body and birth.
Skimming a stream in the vein of the earth,
I float to the brink on the boat of my breath.

Waves of old memories, washes of loss,
lap at the body and scatter again
just where the breathing releases and turns
and leaves us unmoored from the ends of the earth.

Why I Wanted to Play the Cello

All that longing caught between my knees—
to hold with my whole body, and release
the deep unspeakable. Not a lark
transcending life, but here on earth,
rib on ribs, the wood and flesh
vibrato of a rougher chest voice
waking up the heart, a trembling call
for all that's cavernous to hum.

All I wanted was one long note,
to draw the bow across a tautened nerve
sustained enough to touch a tenor
deeper than my words can reach.

And even though my heavy hands
might make the strung hairs growl
like guttered clearings of the throat,
even my most lost and ragged notes,
my clumsy fingers working heavy strings,
was part of reaching for the hollow place
where beauty pulses out of emptiness.

Ode To Falling

I was always good at falling.
When the ligament goes wobbly,
 the ankle turns along the pathway,
only fools try staying upright.
I'd go limp, not do it halfway.

Once upon a time, the Womb-Room—
dim light glowing, pink and pearly,
I stepped forward into nothing,
fell through softness, landed laughing
on velvet-covered foam and batting.

Once, I woke to van doors springing
open, spilling me to bouncing, tumbling
down a California freeway.
"Tuck and roll," a dim voice whispered.
"When you stop, you could be okay."

When I reach that final falling,
let me resist the urge to fight it.
Let me shed my self completely,
gently enter that good nightfall,
tumbling deeper into mystery.

Late Winter Altar, Waiting

Rose quartz and amethyst
pink, yellow, green
though even the pine trees
have browned in these winds

Garland of ivy
tough as old leather
whispers of green coming
after this weather

A battery candlestick
safer than flame
flickers for loved ones
 who watch from their frames

One I am worried for
Two I still miss
Three I will call today
Four for directions
            we're scattered across

May you be happy
May you be safe
May you be well
May we meet in one place

Jayne Brown is the author of *My First Real Tree*, a book of poems published by Foothills Publications. Her poems have appeared in several journals and anthologies including *Calyx, Persimmon Review, Passager,* and *Cider Press Review*. Brown's poem "Finding Her Here" became the title poem for the women's anthology *I am Becoming the Woman I've Wanted*, and was translated into Mandarin and Russian, and commissioned as a choral work by Anna Crusis Women's Chorus.

She received a Master of Fine Arts degree in Creative Writing, Poetry from San Diego State University. She taught college composition and creative writing in California and, after moving to Pennsylvania, at Penn State Berks, until retiring in 2018. Brown was the eighth Poet Laureate of Berks County, Pennsylvania.

www.ingramcontent.com/pod-product-compliance
Lightning Source LLC
LaVergne TN
LVHW090541110826
845146LV00003B/1218

* 9 7 9 8 8 9 9 9 0 3 9 9 1 *